ISLAND OF THE CHILDREN

ISLAND OF THE CHILDREN

CHILDREN

■ *An Anthology of New Poems* ■

COMPILED BY
ANGELA HUTH

DECORATIONS BY
JANE RAY

ORCHARD BOOKS
London

For Eugenie and all children who love poetry

Contents

Foreword

The discovery that there was a certain scarcity of modern poetry for children—most especially young children—came to me when searching for new poems to entertain my daughter, Eugenie. I had been reading her poetry from a very young age, and found that with surprising swiftness we were running out of material. What was plainly missing was a rich anthology of contemporary poetry, written especially for children, by disparate modern poets.

Passionately convinced of this lack, I mooted the idea of just such an anthology to fill the gap. Judith Elliott at Orchard Books reacted with wonderful enthusiasm. So I set about writing to some hundred poets in the British Isles. (Poems arrived, too, from Caribbean, American and Russian writers). I also wrote to various 'secret poets' of my acquaintance: a lawyer, an ex-ambassador, a television critic, a journalist and three writers of children's prose, for instance—people who would not call themselves poets in the strictest sense, and who do not earn their living by poetry, but to whom inspiration sometimes comes.

In equal quantities, poems and encouragement arrived through the post. Many replies came not just with the one or two poems required, but a collection to choose from. Word reached poetry workshops, and some dozen unpublished poets sent their works. In a few cases poets protested they could not (understandably) write to order, or could not write specifically for children. But for the most part the especially requested poems, of many different moods, lengths, subjects and approaches, far exceeded my expectations. The only hard part was making the final choice.

The compiling of *Island of the Children* was altogether a rare and memorable pleasure. Particularly gratifying was the finding of some poets who have been published here and there but who, for inexplicable reasons, have remained unacknowledged talents.

I would like to thank every contributor for his or her time, trouble and diverse inspiration. I know their efforts will delight many a poetry-starved child in the future. And I like to think that, with the arrival of this anthology, the old search for new poetry for the young may—at least for the time being—now be ended.

Angela Huth
Oxford 1987

Foxy Comes to Town

Have you seen the fox in our street
with his rough red hair and his neat sharp feet?

I'd like to hold him, take him in at night
but Dad says he's lousy and Mum says he'd bite.

Sometimes though when I ought to be in bed
I look between my curtains to watch him instead

Creeping on his belly like a soft orange flame.
Then Foxy in the lamplight, I'm glad you're not tame.

Maureen Duffy

An Attempt at Free Verse

People tell you all the time,
Poems do not have to rhyme.
It's often better if they don't
And I'm determined this one won't.
                    Oh dear.

Never mind, I'll start again,
Busy, busy with my pen . . . cil.
I can do it, if I try,
Easy, peasy, pudding and gherkins.

Writing verse is so much fun,
Cheering as the summer weather,
Makes you feel alert and bright,
'Specially when you get it more or less the way you want it.

Wendy Cope

Ever So Cute

(*after A. A. Milne*)

Little boy dressed in his white judo suit,
Little black belt looking ever so cute.
Hush! Hush! Whisper who dares!
Christopher Robin can throw you downstairs.

Go on Mummy, it's only ten —
I want to watch *Dracula's Bride* again.
It's ever so good when he bites ladies' necks —
Me and my teddy like violence and sex.

And when it's over I want to play
The video game we bought today.
Shooting down spaceships. Bleep, bleep, bleep! Kill, kill!
I'll score three million and Dad will get nil.

Little boy growing so sturdy and tough —
Better not argue or he'll cut up rough.
Hush! Hush! Whatever you say,
Christopher Robin will get his own way.

Wendy Cope

King Ezra

King Ezra was a drover
Walked the grey miles to town,
His sceptre was a hazel stick,
A billycock his crown.

His head was whiter than the frost,
His beard white as the floe;
He stood as strong as a stone man
Of Michelangelo.

A sack about his shoulders
In summer and in snow,
And on each foot an army boot
Was splintered at the toe.

Gently he drove the cattle
And softly led the sheep
As he went up to market
Under the Castle Keep.

And if the flock was hasty
Or herd was slow to hand,
He spoke the secret language
All creatures understand.

And never a one would wander
And never a one would stray
As he passed by our window
On Cattle Market Day.

I never heard him call nor cry
Nor saw him strike a blow,
Though in his hand the hazel wand
Was stern as iron crow.

Of all the men to come my way
In days of storm, of calm,
King Ezra wears for me the crown,
King Ezra bears the palm.

I see him as I saw him then
Seasons and worlds ago:
The Good King Ezra whose true name
I never was to know.

Charles Causley

Who is de girl?

who is de girl dat kick de ball
then jump for it over de wall

sallyann is a girl so full-o zest
sallyann is a girl dat just can't rest

who is de girl dat pull de hair
of de bully and make him scare

sallyann is a girl so full-o zest
sallyann is a girl dat just can't rest

who is de girl dat bruise she knee
when she fall from de mango tree

sallyann is a girl so full-o zest
sallyann is a girl dat just can't rest

who is de girl dat set de pace
when boys and girls dem start to race

sallyann is a girl so full-o zest
sallyann is a girl dat just can't rest

John Agard

Ash Talks to Bone

The ghost of a cuckoo
in a skeleton tree
called a promise
to the ghost of me—

a ghostly cuckoo
in a skeleton larch
in doubtful april
or spectral march

take heart, take heart
called the ghostly bird
(or this is what
I thought I heard)

you and I
are ash and bone
you and I
are dead and gone

but seeds are waiting
under all
trees will grow again
strong and tall

deep in the future
centuries past
nuclear night
will end at last

dawn will break
and life rejoice
in unknown words
and a foreign voice

take heart, take heart
called the ghostly bird
(or this was what
I thought I heard)

Joan Aiken

About Words

He
throws the ball to *me*
But I
throw it to *him*. Why?

I and me, him and he—
what a fuss
when there are only two of us!

What is a kiss? if by chance you should get a
scrape or a tumble, a kiss makes you better.
It does for good morning, good bye, or goodnight,
Whatever the greeting, a kiss is all right.
Christmas or birthday, hurray or hello,
it settles an argument, cheers up a woe,
means just the same in French, Spanish, or Greek
Not to be sneezed at, this peck on the cheek!

Postman, postman, bring me a letter
Square and white, the thicker the better.
Postman says: Which one today?
B or C or D or A?

Postman, postman, bring me a note
Bring me a note that somebody wrote!
Postman says: Which one today?
Do or mi, soh, fa, or re?

Perhaps, perhaps
This strange word slips through gaps
Escape from traps,
Is never found
On signs or maps.
Perhaps we'll go to a circus—
Perhaps we shan't . . .
Perhaps we can have a pony—
Perhaps we can't.

Perhaps is just
A word you cannot trust.

Yes is like sunshine after rain
Like finding a seat in a galloping train
Like waking in bed on Christmas day
Like the whirr of the curtain before the play
Like mounting a horse that is ready to run
Yes is the start of all the fun!

Joan Aiken

Power Cut

The lights went out
and everything was still
no light no sight no sound
for fifteen seconds
and then the baby yelled.
We pawed around the dark
and clawed about
to where we thought he fell . . .
Our mother said
"Have we no candle?"
The fire in the stove
made golden bars
where hinges were
and there were sparks
that glittered in the dark
like orange stars.

It was so still.

We groped to windows
to throw the curtains wide
so dark within
and darker still outside
we tried to hide
how weird this darkness feels. . . .
The ghosts of all our ancestors
came creeping through the fields.

Una Leavy

Chicken Brained

In every frozen chicken
You'll find a little bag,
Tucked neatly in the ribcage,
And fastened with a tag.

This extra little parcel
Most thoughtfully contains
Its liver, neck and kidney,
But not its chicken brains.

For the normal farmyard chicken
Is the dumbest bird you'll find
And it's just not worth preserving
Its tiny little mind.

Miles Kington

*P*ostcard From Burma

There's a Burmese maiden on the sand
Beside the Moulmein Bay,
And she doesn't seem to understand
A blooming word I say.

We sat and talked, or so I thought,
Of how I loved her so,
But now it seems I've gone and bought
Her water buffalo.

So it's farewell to the tropic clime,
Goodbye, Rangoon-on-Sea,
And we'll be back in ten days time,
My buffalo and me.

Miles Kington

Fred

I haven't got a dad.
But I'm not sad.
I live with my mum.
My mum's got a boyfriend
—he's real good fun.
His name is Fred.
He drives a lorry.
The lorry's red.
He takes me with him:
we bomb down the road,
we go to a caff,
and then we unload.
He calls me his mate.
I think Fred's great.

Nigel Gray

Friends

I used to feel lonely every night
until my father said,
"What you need is a special friend
you can cuddle in your bed."

First I had a teddy,
then I had a dog,
then I had a panda,
a rabbit and a frog.
Then I had a tiger,
a snake and then a bat,
a lion and an elephant,
a zebra and a cat.

Now my bed is full of friends,
but the problem is, you see,
though none of them feel lonely
there's no room left for me.

Nigel Gray

Day Out

Walking on a low cliff edge,
We watched two seals at sea.
We stared at them—they stared at us,
with expressions of curiosity.
They disappeared and reappeared,
seemed to follow us for a mile or two,
and very soon we began to wonder
just who was watching who.
Perhaps it was *their* day out
and we were exhibits
in their zoo.

Nigel Gray

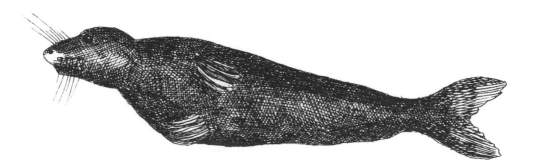

*I*sland of the Children

A man with a silver beard wrote an invitation
To a boy or a girl from every country on earth
To a picnic on his island.
They came, one after the other, one morning.
They were all delighted with the black boy
Because he was black as ebony
And with the Chinese girl
Because she was yellow as starlight
And with the Eskimo boy
Because he was plump and smelt of ice and whales
And with the Greek girl
Because she was honey-coloured
And her words and her breath were like honey too.
The Arab boy
Ran through the fields with the Jewish girl
And their voices mingling
Were like one ancient wise harp of praise.
A girl from Siberia and a boy from Arizona
Had great wonderment
Describing "bear" and "cactus" to one another.
The hundred and fifty children

Delighted in all the animals round them
And the fish and the birds and insects.
It seemed that day would never end
Till the old enchanter
Who had lured them to his island
Sang, "The sun's down!
Time to go home, to get on in the world and
                                        be wise". . . .

The hundred and fifty children
Woke up in scattered beds.
A long long time had passed.
They found themselves the rulers of their countries,
White-haired, grave, and honoured.
They made important speeches
About "freedom", "progress", and "peace".
From time to time they spoke to each other
Across long distances, coldly.
They set spies to spy on all the others.
They had maps with shifting frontiers.
They consulted the maps often.
At last a silver-haired President
Discovered the Island of the Children on his map.
His heart sang like a lark that day.
But it was too late.
A thousand missiles were hurtling here and there.

George Mackay Brown

Dim Dog

He imagines he's invisible,
Head buried in cushions, tail
Splayed like a palm tree,
Impolite end aiming at me.

Dim dog, just because *he*
Is unable to see *me*,
He thinks he's been clever,
Nose twitching, as if scenting a river.

It's only a game though, a lark,
And soon, tiring of the dark,
He swivels, muzzle soft felt,
Butterscotch eyes beginning to melt.

Alan Ross

Collie Romance

Sometimes at night I remember,
Long ago, on an autumn morning,
How she headed for the hills,
Took off without warning.

It was as though, across country,
She'd suddenly received signals,
Sounds unheard by the rest of us,
And had answered without fuss.

When, next day, she returned,
Coat matted, twigs in her fur,
Her look was half guilty, half sated,
Only her eyes burned.

Alan Ross

*W*here's Everybody?

In the cloakroom
Wet coats
Quietly steaming.

In the office
Dinner money
Piled in pounds.

In the head's room
Half a cup
Of cooling tea.

In the corridor
Cupboards
But no crowds.

In the hall
Abandoned
Apparatus.

L B F

In the classrooms
Unread books
And unpushed pencils.

In the infants
Lonely hamster
Wendy House to let.

Deserted plasticene
Still waters
Silent sand.

In the meantime
In the playground . . .
A fire-drill.

Allan Ahlberg

H

The Question

The child stands facing the teacher
(This happens every day)
A small, embarrassed creature
Who can't think what to say.

He gazes up at the ceiling
He stares down at the floor
With a hot and flustered feeling
And a question he can't ignore.

He stands there like the stump of a tree
With a forest of arms around
"It's easy, sir!" "Ask me!" "Ask me!"
The answer, it seems, is found.

The child sits down with a lump in his throat
(This happens everywhere)
And brushes his eyes with the sleeve of his coat
And huddles in his chair.

Allan Ahlberg

Wicked Mrs Bunch

Young Mrs Bunch, a working wife,
Is patient in her labours,
A super mum of spotless life,
Admired by all her neighbours.

Her kittens look so neat and sleek,
And always are well fed.
They go to hear Mass twice a week
To pray for Dad who's dead.

They wash their ears, do household chores,
And never, never swear,
They keep so quiet when they come in,
You wouldn't know they're there.

"How can she cope," the neighbours say,
"Her youngest's only three,
How does she manage, Christmas Day,
For presents on the tree?"

They little know, this cat's a fake,
Head of a school for thieves.
Her kitchen's where each cat must take
Exams before he leaves.

She hangs a jacket on a chair,
With bells sewn on each pocket,
Each cat must take a coin from there,
And then again restock it.

On speech day, when the term is done,
She talks to all the pupils—
"Now you have learnt that thieving's fun,
You need have no more scruples.

"Dress up," she says, "with gloves and spats,
And always be polite,
They think it's rude and nasty cats
Who make their pockets light.

"Save all your rags for begging, lads,
Or scrounging round the doors,
Paint sores and wounds upon your pads,
And ask to do their chores.

"A cat who's handy with his paws
Need never buy a thing,
Thieving can open many doors—
Turn Winter into Spring."

Fiona Pitt-Kethley

A Dog's Tombstone

This tombstone, stranger passing near,
Shows that a little dog lies here:
Tells how a master's loving hand
Carved these words and heaped this sand.
Smile if you please. But, when you die
Shall you be mourned as much as I?

from MacKail's *Selection of Greek Epigrams*.
Translated by The Right Honourable Lord Hailsham

H*en*

Dowdy the Hen
Has nothing to do
But peer and peck, and peck and peer
At nothing.

Sometimes a couple of scratches to right
Sometimes a couple of scratches to left
And sometimes a head-up, red-rimmed stare
At nothing.

A Hen in your pen, O Hen, O when
Will something happen?
Nothing to do but brood on her nest
And wish.

Wish? Wish? What shall she wish for?
Stealthy fingers
Under her bum.
An egg on your dish.

Ted Hughes

Unlucky Steps

To all the people at Victoria Road School, Northwich

Thirteen steps
Leading me down
Down to that big blue door
Big blue door
With a grime-lined face
And a voice like a Polar bear's roar,
The sound of a mechanized blizzard
Which froze my Nikes to the floor

> It sounded like a cloud of poison gas
> Whispering to itself.
> It sounded like a bunch of defrosting cobras
> Slithering off their shelf.

I pushed down the handle
The handle stayed down
For three point five seconds at least
Then the handle sprang back
And the wild white sound
Of a beast that longed to be released
Suddenly stopped.

The silence swelled
As if it were about to burst

My heart felt like a blue iced lolly
    On an ice rink
        In Alaska
            On December the 21st.

I backed up the steps
    13, 12, 11
Away from that cupboard of snows
I backed up the steps
    10, 9, 8, 7
I don't want to join the Eskimos
I backed up the steps
    6, 5, 4
My blood saying: Go man, go man!
I backed up the steps
Then I turned around
That's when I got eaten by a snowman.

                    Adrian Mitchell

Mr Grin and Mr Groan

When Mr Grin and Mr Groan
Sat down at breakfast table
They both ate up the marmalade
As fast as they were able.

They heaped it up upon their toast
Until the pot was through.
Then Mr Grin said cheerfully
"I've had as much as you!"

But Mr Groan stared at his plate
And stiffly stirred his tea,
And looking *very* cross, he said
"You've had as much as me!"

Derwent May

*S*ecrets

"I swear I'll never tell him
— Tell nobody at all.
I promise you can trust me
With secrets big and small.

"So why don't you just tell me?
In a whisper if you like.
And then I'll quite forget it,
And go off on my bike.

"I think you'd *better* tell me
Because, though it's very weird,
The thing about most secrets
Is they're better when they're shared.

"Oh! That's a funny secret!
I never would have guessed.
A really secret secret —
Now, can I hear the rest?

"Gosh, you've got good secrets,
An extraordinary store.
If you feel you've got too many
You can always tell me more."

Two days later . . .
"Why are you so cross with me?
What's it all about?
Well, I only told *one* person —
He must have let it out!

"I swear I'll never tell again,
I've learnt that lesson well:
If you mean to keep a secret
You simply mustn't tell . . . anyone."

Augusta Skye

Bye Now   Goodbye Now

Walk good   Walk well
   Walk good   Walk well
Noh mek macca go juk yu   Don't let thorns run in you
Or cow go buck yu.   Or let a cow butt you.
Noh mek dog bite yu   Don't let a dog bite you
Or hungry go ketch yu, yah!   Or hunger catch you, hear!

Noh mek sunhot turn yu dry.   Don't let sun's heat turn you dry.
Noh mek rain soak yu.   Don't let rain soak you.
Noh mek tief tief yu   Don't let a thief rob you
Or stone go buck yu foot, yah! Or a stone bump your foot, hear!
   Walk good   Walk well
     Walk good   Walk well

James Berry

Sally's Alphabet

A is for alphabet
B is for boy
C is for cat, if you like

    but cats can't learn letters
    and all boys enjoy
    racing downhill on a bike

D is for donkey
E is for egg
F is a fairly big fish

    but donkeys don't swim
    and a fish wouldn't eat
    two hard-boiled eggs on a dish

G is a girl, and
Home is a place
I is for ink, I should think

    but girls who go home
    with ink on their face
    must scrub themselves clean in the sink

J is for Jennifer
K is for King
L is a lizard that's green

    so Jennifer once
    took her lizard along
    to wave at the King and the Queen

M is a mouse
N is a newt
O is an ostrich, for sure

    they live in a house
    where they sing to a flute
    as they sit in a ring on the floor

P is for pepper
Q is a queue
R is a big roundabout

but pepper could make
a whole queue go "Atchoo!"
and rush round and round to get out

S is a suit, and
T is a tailor
U is an uncle who's old

he went off to bed
with a needle and thread
to sew up some cloth made of gold

V is a vegetable
W a whale
X is a kind of a cross

but whales who eat vegetables
with a big meal
get pains as they pitch and they toss

Y is a yawn
Z is zig-zag
A takes us back to the start

and you're yawning, my love
as you zig-zag to bed
so Goodnight and God bless you sweetheart

Edwin Brock

*T*hree Girls and a Romple

Three little girls
    as little girls do
Decided to look for
    a Romple
For one of them said
    she once knew a boy who
Saw a baby one out with
    its uncle

They started by asking
    anyone
Who might know what a Romple
    was like
What a Romple would say
    if you saw him one day
Riding no-hands on his
    bike

Someone said Romples were
    usually blue
Someone said Romples were
    small
Another one said that
    as far as he knew
There weren't any Romples
    at all

But Sally said Romples are
    weaselly things
And Hannah said Romples are
    fat
And Klos said a Romple has
    very small wings
Which he carries around in
    his hat

An owl in a tree hooted
    listen to me
I've told you again
    and again
Romples are funny
    they hide when it's sunny
And only come out
    in the rain

The ducks said they quack
  and the dogs said they bark
And a very small girl
  in a pram
Said they're covered in hairs
  like the best Teddy Bears
And they're nearly as big
  as I am

But Sally said Romples are
  weaselly things
And Hannah said Romples are
  fat
And Klos said a Romple has
  very small wings
Which he carries around in
  his hat

So three little girls
  as little girls do
Decided to go home
  to bed
And one day next week
  when they play hide and seek
They'll look for a Whatsit
  instead.

Edwin Brock

Catherine's Poem

"Aren't poems like your toys, Daddy?"
Catherine said.
"And didn't you and Mammy make me
And God made the thread?"

Seamus Heaney

Good Questions. Bad Answers.

Where's the rattle
I shook
when I was 1?
Vanished

Where's the Teddy
I hugged
when I was 2?
Lost

Where's the sand box
I played in
when I was 3?
Broken up

Where's the beach ball
I kicked
when I was 4?
Burst

Where's the fort
I built
when I was 5?
Destroyed

Where's the box of comics
I collected
when I was 6?
Missing

Where's the electric train set
I loved
when I was 7?
Given away

Where's the holiday scrap book
I made
when I was 8?
   Disappeared

Where's the tin of marbles
I had
when I was 9?
   Swopped

Where's the bicycle
I rode
when I was 10?
   Sold

What, gone? Everything?
Yes, all gone,
all gone . . . .

                                   Wes Magee

Until Gran Died

The minnows I caught
lived for a few days in a jar
then floated side-up on the surface.
We buried them beneath the hedge.
I didn't cry, but felt sad inside.

I thought
I could deal with funerals,
that is until gran died.

The goldfish I kept in a bowl
passed away with old age.
Mum wrapped him in newspaper
and we buried him next to a rose bush.
I didn't cry, but felt sad inside.

I thought
I could deal with funerals,
that is until gran died.

My cat lay stiff in a shoe box
after being hit by a car.
Dad dug a hole and we buried her
under the apple tree.
I didn't cry, but felt very sad inside.

 I thought
 I could deal with funerals,
 that is until gran died.

And when she died
I went to the funeral
with relations dressed in black.
They cried, and so did I.
Salty tears ran down my face. Oh, how I cried.

 Yes, I thought
 I could deal with funerals,
 that is until gran died.

She was buried beside an old church
and even the sky wept that day.
Rain fell and fell and fell,
and thunder sobbed far away across the town.
I cried and I cried.

 I thought
 I could deal with funerals,
 that is until gran
 died.

Wes Magee

Midnight

Riddle me over
in white and red clover,
call down the stars from the sky,
let the owl scratch
on the farmer's thatch
and the streams and the rivers run dry.

The full moon is bright
on this starry night,
a frog wears a jewel in its head,
the magic stone
that I seek alone
is aquamarine and red.

I hear a black bat
and a tiger-eyed cat
flitting about in the dark.
Now it is late,
a hand lifts the gate,
and the farmdog begins to bark.

Jeremy Reed

Transitional

Clusters of elder jet the lane
where hoverflies lazily drone;
plantain's produced a yellow ruff
of seeds around a chocolate cone,
dust's filmed the blackberry, a thrush
spikes purple from that bramble bush.

I disappear across country,
the stillness takes me out of time,
the saffron chestnut leaf contends
with auburn sycamore and lime.
The squirrel's secret, it will roll
a nut-store into its tree hole.

I walk between the two seasons,
each leaf's a transitional edge,
falling on the side of winter;
splotchy plane leaves have starred the hedge.
The oak is thinning, its gold crown
deckles to orange, ochre, brown.

Jeremy Reed

Berries

Now is the time of berries waxing fat,
the scarlet of hawthorn and bryony,
the mauve granulations of blackberry,
the elder's pitch, grape-black of a wine vat.

I walk the hedgerows, the blueish blackthorn
is dusted lilac, and here bittersweet
clashes with garish cuckoopint. Birds eat
the haws; crows linger in the stubbled corn.

Festoons of bindweed froth the brambled lane,
the honeysuckle's berried a red crown
by low oak-sprays deckled a sherry-brown,
the colour of chestnuts brought down by rain.

Jeremy Reed

Gulls Playing

The day was so dull
That I went for a walk,
A walk on the chalk
Of the high cliffs of Dover.
When I looked over
Them, scared I should fall
(For chalky cliffs crumble,
It's too far to tumble)
I made myself safe
Standing carefully back,
Looked across at a crack
Or a gap in the cliff
And life became full
Of remarkable things.

I saw that a gull
Can fly without wings.
Could glide on the airs
As long as it cares
To (I mean with no flap,
Thin airs hold it up.)
On a day without sun
Gulls having fun.

Cliffs the colour of sheep,
Gulls the colour of snow,
Over the sea so grey and deep,
Up to the cliffs so tall and steep,
The white gulls flow.

When swimmers compete
They push with their feet
At the end of the pool
And swim back, as the gull
(Win or lose, doesn't care)
Skimming through air
Taps the cliff with its bill
Or its wingtip and swerves
Back over grey waves.

Then glides in again,
Out again, in:
Not looking for food,
And not to be good,
And not to show off,
It plays tag with the cliff.

And so when I'm dull,
Or Simple like Simon,
I think of the gull
Climbing the air,
The air we all share,
Using the air
To have a good time on.

Cliffs the colour of sheep,
Gulls the colour of snow,
Over the sea so grey and deep,
Up to the cliffs so tall and steep
The white gulls flow.

P. J. Kavanagh

*P*laying Alone

"What can I do?"
Is Marjorie's moan.
She's been a bus
And drawn a door,
And on the floor
Fenced round two
Ducklings and one
Rhinoceros.

"Well, send the beast
And those that quack
Aboard the bus
Out through the door
For a quiet tour.
You've proved at least
Ducks don't attack
Rhinoceros."

How like a man
(Thinks Marjorie)
To glance up from
His book and make
Such daft remarks,
And put no plan
To save poor me
From tedium!

Roy Fuller

I Bet You Didn't Know That

When elephants look in a mirror
They feel so disgustingly fat,
They put on their trunks and go jogging.
            I bet you didn't know that.

What goes through the mind of a mackerel
Before sitting down to a sprat?
"It's true what they say — small is lovely."
            I bet you didn't know that.

When not being dirty on telly,
The pig wipes his feet on the mat
And goes round his sty with a hoover.
            I bet you didn't know that.

The hermit-crab, true to her nature,
Likes wearing a whelk for a hat
And showing her passion for fashion.
            I bet you didn't know that.

The crocodile can't sing for toffee,

Except in the key of B flat,

That's why he appears to be crying.

       I bet you didn't know that.

A mouse that is crazy for cricket

Is commonly known as a bat:

The umpire is really a vampire.

       I bet you didn't know *that*.

Roger Woddis

From My Window

The waters fall in rectangles

Cities sprout umbrellas

Clear water paints a blurred picture

Tears slide from afternoon branches

Dirt breathes a deep sigh of mud

It's raining today

Zaro Weil

*H*ow To Get An Idea

Dig into mud
> or

Open up a new box of crayons
> or

Run your fingers through a bag of marbles
> or

Skip a stone across water
> or

Ask a cat to lend you one
> or

Stand quietly under a dictionary
> or

Stick out your tongue and say, "Ah!"
> or

Put an empty picture frame on the wall and wait

Zaro Weil

What Does The Shopping Spider Say?

What does the Shopping Spider say
    When she wishes to buy some bread?
Have you ever heard one single word
    A Shopping Spider has said?

I can tell you. She lifts up her long legs
    As she enters the Village shop
And without a word said she removes the bread
    and a very small lollipop.

Then the Old Shopkeeper says: "Madam,
    I know it is rather absurd
But how can I tell what you wish me to sell
    If you never utter a word?"

George Barker

The Saga of Baba Yaga

Baba Yaga is a witch.
In olden days when she was poor
She'd sit by the fire and scratch and twitch,
Poke the logs and spit and choke
Get up every minute to open the door
To let out clouds of thick black smoke.

Hearing her cough and sniffle and sigh
The Prince of Darkness sent a present
Drawn through the blood-red evening sky
By two hundred brace of pheasant
Who installed it by and by —
While Baba Yaga was out looking
For wood that wasn't green or new
With which to do her nightly cooking
That wouldn't smoke, or burn her stew.

Baba Yaga came home late
With little wood but full of hate
As she fumbled at her gate.
She went inside and kicked the cat
Who turned its back on her and spat.
So next she leapt towards her goat
And caught it neatly by the throat —
Till she saw so large and black
A sight which made her grip go slack.

Now Baba Yaga wears a dress
Washes once a week — more or less —
Sits at the table drinking lager;
And when she's going to a coven
Just puts her meat into the oven —
For Baba Yaga has an Aga!
A stove for cooking cakes and pies
That never blacks her narrow eyes.

Baba Yaga likes the change
To a shining kitchen range.
In winter she'll put on her bonnet
Light a pipe and climb up on it
While her goat stays down below
Dancing neither quick nor slow
For its mistress Baba Yaga —
Who takes her pen and writes a saga,
Sitting cross-legged on her Aga.

Life is better with an Aga —
Says the cat of Baba Yaga
Which, sitting by the oven door
Sips its lager through a straw.

Alan Sillitoe

Monkey

Have you ever watched a monkey
Climbing up a tree?
He can reach the tip-most top-most
Before you count to three.
And those who try to catch him
Just haven't got a chance.
Off he goes like a man in space
A monkey grin on his monkey face,
Legs and tail all over the place
And lands on another branch.

A cow may moo and a bee may buzz
But none can jump like a monkey does!

Herbert Kretzmer

Yakkity Yak

Yakkity Yak was a shaggy old yak
Who lived in high Tibet
He truly was the hairiest yak
That you have ever met.
He had hair from his toes
To the tip of his nose,
So his toes never froze
In the wintery snows.
He had hair where hair
Never usually grows,
Had Yakkity Yak.

No other beast in the faraway East
Had seen his like before.
A grizzly bear may have plenty of hair,
But Yakkity Yak had more.
He had hair overflowing,
And hair underneath.
It grew like the heather
That grows on the heath.
It even took root
On the lily-white teeth
Of Yakkity Yak!

Travellers came from everywhere,
They came by sea and they came by air
To gawp and gape and glare and stare
At Yakkity Yak and his beautiful hair.

And while they were there
They stole bits of his hair
To show their kith and kin.
They cut and they snipped
'Til they finally stripped
Old Yakkity to the skin.

Picture poor Yakkity stripped of his hair.
Shivering, quivering, lonely and bare
At the end of his days there was no one to care
For Yakkity Yak . . .

If only the tourists had taken their snaps
Instead of those snips of hair,
Yakkity Yak the shaggy old yak
Would certainly still be there.

And we could have taken that journey
And back
And seen him walking tall.
Yakkity Yak the shaggy old yak,
The shaggiest yak of them all!

Herbert Kretzmer

The Jamjar's Song

Wash me clean, unpeel my skin,
keep me to keep your nowt-much in.
Tie a string around my neck,
dip me in deep bluegreen.
Fill me full of living fullstops
and watch them till they hatch
into wriggling, swimming commas.

Let me flip my lid and catch
the buzz of a summer afternoon.
Before it goes insane,
be God: set it free again.
I'm a keen collector of anything:
barley, buttons, biros, broken
necklaces of rain . . .
Run your fingertip round my rim
and make me sing,
fill me up and up and up
till I overflow my brim.
I know I'm not what I was
when I was a jar of jam,
but you won't throw me out because
I am what I am.

Brian McCabe

A *Woobit Song*

A Woobit went walking through Carraway Town
In his ragged new sweater and his tin golden crown.
He whiffled and wurbled and sang "worrajee",
Because he was coming to eat me for tea.

He woffed on the doorstep and wonged on the bell,
He sniggled and snorfed at the thought of the smell
Of little girl chops and little girl pies,
(He wanted to crunch me with vinegary fries).

But I didn't care for his scrobbles and squeals,
(Because *nobody* likes to be Woobitses' meals),
So I tromped on his crown, and wurfulled his sweater,
And now (for a Woobit) he couldn't be better.

Lucy Coats

Cat-English

It may seem funny, but my cat
Is learning English. Think of that!
For years she did all right with "Meow",
But that won't satisfy her now,
And where before she'd squawk or squeak
She'll try with all her might to speak.
So when I came downstairs today
I was impressed to hear her say
"Hallo". Not like a person, true;
It might not sound quite right to you,
More of a simple squeak or squawk—
Still, that's what happens when cats talk:
Their mouths and tongues and things are fine,
But different shapes from yours and mine;
They simply try their level best
And our good will must do the rest.
So when I pick up Sarah's dish
And ask who's for a spot of fish,
I have to listen carefully,
But I've no doubt she answers "Me!"

And when I serve her with the stuff
It's "Ta" she tells me, right enough.
Well now, I could go on about
Her call of "Bye!" when I go out
And "Hi!" when I come home again,
But by this stage the point is plain:
If you've a sympathetic ear
Cat-English comes through loud and clear;
Of course, the words are short and few,
The accent strange, and strident too,
And our side never gets a crack
At any kind of answer back,
But think of it the other way,
With them to listen, you to say.
Imagine the unholy row
You'd make with "Mew!" and "Purr!" and "Meow!"
And not get anything across!
Sarah would give her head a toss,
Her nose or tail a scornful twitch—
I really cannot settle which—
And gaze at you in sad distress
For such pathetic childishness.
Unless you want a snub like that
Leave all the talking to your cat.

Kingsley Amis

S*kylark*

skylark skylark soaring high
beware the dark atomic dust
which comes with neither shape nor warning
which comes with neither sound nor savour
skylark skylark soaring high

skylark skylark soaring high
beware the dark atomic dust
it will suck flight from your wings and
sap the rhythm of your heartbeat
skylark skylark soaring high

skylark skylark soaring high
beware the dark atomic dust
in its place it is no menace
undisturbed it's no destroyer
skylark skylark soaring high

skylark skylark soaring high
beware the dark atomic dust
it was i who pulled the trigger
now my guilt is my own wounding
skylark skylark soaring high

skylark skylark soaring high
beware the dark atomic dust
my royal brother gave the order
lasting peace was all he wanted
skylark skylark soaring high

skylark skylark all aglow
no longer can i see you fly
since the cloud has burnt my vision
are you climbing are you falling
skylark skylark all aglow

Aonghas MacNeacail

Old Echo

Cousin Jonathan came to stay.
I can't stand him. Never could.
Tawny eyes as sharp as needles.
Picks and pokes and prods at his food.

Smirked and sniggered when I told him
I believe in ghouls and ghosts.
He's not as brainy as he thinks.
He's thicker than two football posts.

Dad talks to a ghost each day
And he says he's kind and wise.
Lives in a chalkpit under the hill
And listens to Dad and gives him advice.

Old Echo I call him. So does Dad.
Jonathan said, "He doesn't exist.
You made him up, you silly fat fool."
Closed his hand, hardened his fist.

"He does," I shouted. "I know he does."
I took Jonathan down to the pit.
All the way he scoffed and sneered.
"Aren't you brave! Aren't you frit?"

I was a bit and that's right to be
Or you could come a real cropper.
Dad says ghosts are poor lost souls.
"Be sure," he says, "and treat them proper."

Led my cousin straight through the nettles.
It was hot down there, and ever so still.
Heard the humming of hundreds of bees,
A dog barking up on the hill.

"Well! where is he?" Jonathan said.
Swiped the nettles, swished at the air.
"I told you so. He doesn't exist.
There isn't a ghost at all, is there?"

"Is there? Is there?" said Old Echo.
Jonathan tossed like a furious bull.
Hopped and sniggered and yelled back,
"Old Echo, you're a silly fool."

"You're a silly fool," answered Old Echo.
My cousin's face turned blotchy and red.
Pawed the air, stamped on the nettles.
"What? What did you call me?" he said.

"A very silly little fool!
That's what I said," Old Echo replied.
Jonathan's eyes went glassy as marbles.
Jonathan looped the loop inside.

Jonathan scrammed away from the pit
White as chalk and green as cheese.
Blubbed all night and then next morning
Blew back home to his mum on the breeze.

Kevin Crossley-Holland

*T*o His Daughter In The Wars
27.10.86

Your front wheel runs ahead of you

Through the yew tree tunnels.

The yew berries lie in your path like beads

For you to thread. You jammed your brakes

And flew ahead of your plans

To make yew berry chains.

Your elbows were grazed.

Your handlebars were askew.

Someone had to straighten them for you.

Hugo Williams

The Evil Adults

We took the *Evil Adults* in the middle of the night.
We swooped upon their houses
they came without a fight.
For we were many thousands and they were twenty-two.
We walked them through the cheering crowds
and locked them in the zoo.
Four of them were Teachers,
Six of them were Mums,
Eight of them were Fathers . . . stop
let me do my sums . . .
Two were Politicians,
Three were cruel and mean,
and one had just invented an anti-child machine.

We put them in the Tiger cage,
The tigers didn't mind,
they ate the *Evil Adults* . . . man and woman kind.
Grown-ups of this town be warned,
We are watching you,
Treat your children kindly,
Or you know what we will do.

Sue Townsend

89

My Dad

I love to watch my Dad
when he's cutting his toenails.
my Dad does not mind
if he has an audience.
He is like a medical T.V. show
during a tricky operation.
He says, "First you trim the nail
leaving a strip of white at the top
before probing under the nail for crud."
The crud is all different colours
because it is fluff from his socks.
He cannot understand people
who think that's all there is
to cutting your nails.
Neither can I.

Next he wedges a tiny pair of silver scissors
into the corner and takes another scissors
and goes clip, clip, clip.
That's for in-grown toenails.
To polish things off,
he scrapes the sides of his nail
with a little file just in case.
I would like to be as skilled
as my Dad at cutting toenails
in the years to come.

Julie O'Callaghan

Hedgehog's Classroom

The Gray Kitten sits at the front
with a dunce-hat on her head.
Squirrel fires a spit-ball
from the fourth row back
which misses Ferret's head by a millimetre.
Rat is rooting in his desk
for the last piece of cheese he has stashed
and the Calico Kitten is twitching
his whiskers and flapping his ears,
trying to make the dunce laugh.
Hedgehog looks through his glasses,
past his class notes, and waves
his wooden pointer as a threat:
"Rat, please stand up and explain
to us what you have in your desk
that has kept your attention
from my lesson for ten solid minutes."
With this diversion, Ferret passes a note
to Black Kitten which says,
"Are you going hunting after school?
If so, can I come with you, please say yes."

The Black Kitten's mouth forms one word: "No."
The wooden pointer arrives at his face:
"Ferret and Black Kitten 100 times for tomorrow—
I will not pass notes in class."

Julie O'Callaghan

Answers

1.

As I grow old and just a trifle frayed,
It's nice to know that I have sometimes made
You children and occasionally the staff
Stop work and have instead a little laugh.

2.

Dear children, far across the sea,
How good of you to write to me.
I love to read the things you say
When you are miles and miles away.
Young people, and I think I'm right,
Are nicer when they're out of sight.

3.
From far and near, from near and far,
Your letters come. How kind you are!
I cannot, as I'm sure you know,
Write back to all of you, and so
Instead I send (and that's what this is)
Lots and lots of love and kisses.

Roald Dahl

Roald Dahl receives thousands of letters from children all over the world. These poems are from a selection of his replies.   A.H.

I Wish I Were a Wood-Louse

I wish I were a wood-louse,
  In a green, mossy house,
Under a big flat stone:
  I would roll into a ball
  When people came to call,
And then they would leave me alone.

To be a centipede
Would be very nice indeed,
If I had fifty pairs of boots:
Or an owl in a hollow tree,
Singing "Nobody cares for me,
And I don't care two hoots."

Bright Robin Redbreast
In a kettle built his nest,
Beneath the wide, windy skies:
What does he like to eat
For his Christmas treat?
Worm pudding, and squashed flies.

John Heath-Stubbs

*T*he *Witch*

Judy Cracko—she was a witch,
And lived in a muddy, smelly ditch:

But when the moon shone bright, she'd fly
On a tatty old broomstick, up in the sky,

With the bats, and the owls, and the booboo birds,
Shouting out loud the most horrible words,

Like Botheration, and Bottom, and Belly,
And Nurts and Nark it and Not on your Nelly!

Now the judge, Mr Justice Fuzzywig,
And the village policeman, Constable Pigg,

And Major Wilberforce Wotherspoon,
And a lady called Miss Prissy La Prune,

Put their heads together, and vowed
That sort of behaviour should not be allowed.

So they locked her up in a dungeon dim
With her one-eyed pussycat, Smoky Jim.

But she didn't stay long in that prison cell—
She muttered a rather difficult spell:

Then seven red devils, with horns and tails,
And seldom manicured fingernails,

And each with one great donkey's hoof,
Whirled Judy and Jim through a hole in the roof,

Over the seas and far away
To an island eastward of Cathay:
She's living there still, to this very day.

John Heath-Stubbs

Grandmother's ring

When, in the dark, old-fashioned street
of bungalows, a neighbour enquired
after my Gran, I tried to sound mature
but failed. My ten-years voice splintered
as I summonsed up the words "she died last night".

She left me a hideous ring.
It was laid away in velveteen, in some
secret place, to await 'the future'
and forgotten. But, as I breezed
away my teens, something strange occurred:

It transformed like a chrysalis into a butterfly.
(Or perhaps it was I who'd changed?)
We took it out the day of my engagement: It was
exquisite. In the jeweller's shop
where I was scared to cough

my clothes all scruffed, he looked at me
in some disdain, then peered down his inch-long
telescope. And grew excited. Well, as much as such
sombre grey-legs ever dare. He called his student "Look,
such rare, perfect colour!" then turned to me, began "My dear . . . "

She's laughing now. I can see her bloomers
(pink, with frills) wrapped around her laughing thighs.
I can visualise the slant-ceiling
of the attic room where she and I
sat for hours making stories, poems, rhymes:

She left me, too, a love of complicated sounds, and tales
of high adventure. Of musical words,
and made up scraps of nonsense.
So years on, when she had died, and I
was old enough to choose, she made me write.

Not doctor, or teach, or engineer.
And having made sure I'd always be poor,
she left me a ring worth a fortune. Sapphires and diamonds
shoved in my pocket, I walked home,
half-laughing through the pricking tears. How did she know?

Kathleen Jamie

Leopard

When the leopard came out in spots
No one would believe she was unwell.
"Don't waste my time," the vet complained,
While her friends the lynx and jaguar
Agreed she was a dreadful pain:
"Spots? Hasn't she heard? She's *supposed* . . ."

But the leopard drained away.
Her oily joints seized up.
Her claws wouldn't slide on their runners.
Her coat's satin was sanded to matt.
She lay in the woodfern, spots before her eyes,
Spots of darkness, more spots than the spots of night.

Blake Morrison

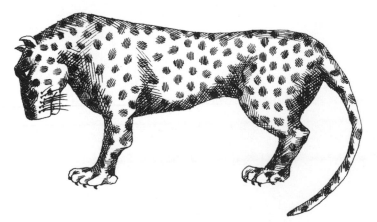

St Francis of Assisi

St Francis of Assisi
Who had never heard of ecology
Loved birds and beasts and flowers
All the same. He spent his hours
In prayer and contemplation,
Believing that God's Creation
Covered all things, great and small.
St Francis knew that every animal
And plant has a right to life and space
And that each one has its certain place
Among the other million trillions.
Nowadays, clever people like Oxford dons
Explain that natural stability
Is linked to biological diversity
And that mankind's own future depends
On how we treat our feathered friends.
Ecology, they seem to say,
Is just self-interest put another way.
I wonder what St Francis would have thought
About arguments of this sort.

Stanley Johnson

There Once Was a Pismire

There once was a pismire,*
And he had his house
Among silvery boughs.
His friend the nightingale
Nested in the galingale†
Down by the quagmire.
The small, velvet-coated
Blind mouldywarp's
Home was the dome
Of a skirling starling.
On both the friends he doted:
"I'll leave my closet,"
He said, "and I'll visit
Those two, and I'll hear
Them sing a motet
Both loud and clear,
With flats and sharps,
As a duet."

Eugene Dubnov

Translated from the Russian by John Heath-Stubbs
* a pismire is an ant   † galingale is a plant also called water-sedge

A *Funny Thing Happened*

As we were coming to school today on our school bus
Our driver had an AAAARGGHH!
        BBLLUPFPFTTT!
            CCCCCRRRRRUUUUUNNNNNCCCCCHHHHH!
             BANGZAPSMASHPOWSPLATDOINGTHUDGERK!
accident with a HIPPOPOTAMUS.

It looked like there were hippo-bits from here
                to Minnesota—
When we put them all together, what we got was a
            MUS-HIP-POP-OTA.

We thought we ought to have one more go before restarting
                our trip—
This time we ended up with a POP-MUS-OTA-HIP.

We were all begining to wish we'd never bothered to stop
When at the very next attempt we made an OTA-HIP-MUS-POP.

So we climbed back on board, and from the rear of the bus
We saw all four waving—the HIP, the POP, the OTA and the
MUS.

And we all waved back until the POP and the MUS and the HIP
and the OTA—
They each grew remoter
and remoter
and remoter
and remoter.

David Horner

Bear

The bear sat under the Christmas tree
making laws
and his paws
had nails as black as black could be.

The star that glistened in the sky
knew not why
the bear sat under the Christmas tree
making laws
and his paws
had nails as black as black could be.

The angel over the Christmas tree
sang *do ray me*,
so sang he,
but the star that glistened in the sky
knew not why
the angel over the Christmas tree
sang *do ray me*,
so sang he,
and the bear sat under the Christmas tree
making laws
and his paws
had nails as black as black could be.

It got so late in the afternoon
that the sky got dark very much too soon,
but the bear sat under the Christmas tree
making laws
and his paws
had nails as black as black could be.

And the laws he made which nobody knows
said the moon had a very long greenish nose,
so the moon turned yellow with a long green nose
and you can see if you get free
that the moon has a long green nose and he
loves the angel on the Christmas tree,
and the star that glistens in the sky,
and the bear and his paws with an amorous sigh
and the clouds that are passing by on high.

Peter Levi

Me And My Bruv

Me an my bruv get along just great,
My bruv's twelve and I'm nearly eight;
We support United, my bruv and me,
And clock all the football on the TV.
My bruv's at big school, he does French and Maths;
When I show him my News, my bruv laughs.
We like beef-burglars, oven chips and peas,
That's me and my bruv's favourite teas.
We don't like homework, my bruv gets tons;
Even my bruv can't do my sums.
My bruv collects things, real antiques,
And tapes and comics, he's got heaps.
Bruv's into software, that means games;
Doing the computer really takes brains.
Our mum says my bruv's a big lazy lump,
And me and my bruv's room's a rubbish dump.
It's half his mess, but he blames me, still—
I luv my bruv, my bruv's mega-brill!

Stephen Mulrine

Spiders

What makes a spider do his thing
Of weaving bits of see-through string
That float away in air?
They say that all his enterprise
Is just to catch the buzzing flies
And eat them in his lair.

Yet sometimes, in the misty haze
When early morning's slanting rays
First carry in the dawn,
A myriad spiders work away
Between the blades of grass to lay
A carpet on the lawn.

Then you can walk with sliding feet
Upon the silver, silken sheet
Which they have made for you
And friends who come around to play
Quite easily can track your way
Across the shining dew.

I like the careful spider best
Who spins at night-time without rest
To meet the next day's needs;
He seems to read some blue-print plan
To stretch his geometric span
Above the flowers and weeds.

Then, when the morning shower has stopped
You'll think the careless clouds have dropped
Some treasure in their flight;
For there, between the roses strung,
The multi-spangled threads are hung
With diamonds full of light.

Some other larger spiders weave
Strong nets that catch and hold your sleeve
And give you such a fright,
You tear the clinging web apart
For fear the owner at its heart
Will spring at you and bite.

Then broken filaments, pulled free,
Go drifting over land and sea
Towards the sunset sky
To reach that Giant-Spider Land
Where in the rocks and caverns stand
Black monsters ten foot high.

A spider in our homely world
Is small and weak and lies close-curled
When held inside your hand
Until he feels the moment's come
To abseil gently from your thumb
On one transparent strand.

Sir Fred Warner

Feeling Hungry

When you feeling hungry
time can go by so slowly
like when I'm out shopping
with me Mum

I say, "I'm hungry"
She says, "You've just eaten"

I say again, "I'm hungry"
She says again, "You've just eaten"

"Well, I don't know, it must be the cold
but me belly feel like a dough-nut with a hole"

Grace Nichols

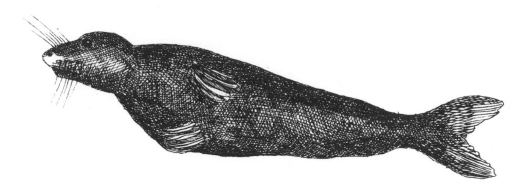

Mary and Sarah

Mary likes smooth things,
Things that glide:
Sleek skis swishing down a mountainside.

Sarah likes rough things,
Things that snatch:
Boats with barnacled bottoms, thatch.

Mary likes smooth things,
Things all mellow:
Milk, silk, runny honey, tunes on a cello.

Sarah likes rough things,
Things all troubly:
Crags, snags, bristles, thistles, fields left stubbly.

Mary says—polish,
Sarah says—rust,
Mary says—mayonnaise,
Sarah says—crust.

Sarah says—hedgehogs,
Mary says—seals,
Sarah says—sticklebacks,
Mary says—eels.

Give me, says Mary,
The slide of a stream,
The touch of a petal,
A bowl of ice-cream.

Give me, says Sarah,
The gales of a coast,
The husk of a chestnut,
A plate of burnt toast . . .

Mary and Sarah—
They'll never agree
Till peaches and coconuts
Grow on one tree.

Richard Edwards

Eugenie and the Ice

It grew cold. Puddles froze
And the wind like a knife
Swept out of Siberia
Chilling the life
Of the blackbird, the starling,
The sparrow, the crow,
And burying fields
Under blank sheets of snow.

It grew colder. The streams
Turned as solid as stone;
White waterfalls fanged
As if carved out of bone;
The lapwing, the wagtail,
The dipper all flew
To feed by the sea —
Then the sea froze too.

"It's *too* cold!" said Eugenie,
And marching outside,
She strode down to the edge
Of the desolate tide,
Where she faced the cruel wind
With a shake of her fist
Shouting, "Shoo! Scram! Skidaddle!
Buzz off! I insist!"

Well, the wind didn't wait
To be shouted at twice,
It turned tail and fled home
While, in place of the ice,
Water warmed, water woke,
Water gurgled and gushed,
Water spouted and sparkled
And rippled and rushed.

And the birds! How they sang!
From the heron's sharp bill
Came a croak of delight,
From the wren came a trill,
And a turtle dove purred
On each branch of each tree
As Eugenie walked home
From the blue-again sea.

Richard Edwards

To Pass the Time

When I'm bored I count things:
Cornflakes, cars,
Pencils, people, leaves on trees,
Raindrops, stars,
Footsteps, heartbeats, pebbles, waves,
Gaggles, herds and flocks,
Freckles, blinks per minute,
The ticks
Of clocks.

Eighty-seven lamp-posts
Line our street.
Did you know a wood-louse has
Fourteen feet?
And — two vests, four pairs of pants, six shirts, two
T-shirts, one pair of jeans, two other pairs of trousers,
one pair of shorts, three belts, three pullovers, one of
them without sleeves, a raincoat, a jacket, two pairs of
pyjamas, one glove, one tie and eleven socks are —
The clothes I've got
In five drawers and one wardrobe:
I'm bored
A lot.

Richard Edwards

James and Mrs Curry

A carrot called James—
Yes, carrots have names—
Looked up from the veg patch and wondered
Why plump Mrs Curry
Seemed in such a hurry
As down through the garden she thundered.

Between the broad beans
And trembling greens
That shrank from her merciless stride,
She moved like an arrow
Past leek, sprout and marrow
To suddenly stop at James' side.

"I thought it looked fine,
That boiled beef of mine,
But no, it needs carrots," she muttered.
"At least just the one,
Cooked briskly till done
To a turn and then lavishly buttered."

With that she bent low
And, choosing James' row,
Grabbed hold of his feathery top
To jump like a kitten
That thinks it's been bitten
When James cried out angrily: "Stop!"

"Hands off or I'll thump you,
I'll batter you, bump you,
And, struggling as hard as I'm able,
Put up a fierce fight
With all of my might
From here to the dining room table!"

Poor woman. What squeals!
She took to her heels
And fled away, stammering, "S-s-s-s-save me!"
And never since then
Served carrots again,
Just dunked soggy bread in her gravy.

Richard Edwards

Oh, To Be . . .

"Oh, to be an eagle
And to swoop down from a peak
With the golden sunlight flashing
From the fierce hook of my beak;

"Oh, to be an eagle
And to terrify the sky
With a beat of wings like thunder
And a wild, barbaric cry;

"Oh . . . but why keep dreaming?
I must learn to be myself,"
Said the rubber duckling sadly
On its soapy bathroom shelf.

Richard Edwards

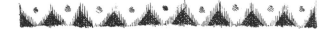

Lonely Violet

Lonely Violet wept for years
On her misty Highland hill,
Tears and tears and tears and tears,
Buckets of them, floods, until
All her rooms were waterlogged,
Everything so soaked and sogged
That the rising tide of water
Trapped the Highlands' hapless daughter
Up inside the tiny loft
Of her overflowing croft.

Luckily a local laddie,
Known as something of a loon,
Jolly James McGilliegaddy,
Joker, comic, clown, buffoon,
Heartiest of Scottish hearties,
Life and soul of Highland parties,
In the nick of time rode by,
Cracked a joke and rescued Vi
From her wet and wobbly rafter
With a ladder made of laughter . . .

They lived happily ever after.
Richard Edwards

Index of Poets and First Lines